HAPPY NOTES!

101 Sticky Note Surpri[ses] to Make You Smile

 Sourcebooks, Inc.®
Naperville, Illinois

Make Someone Smile TODAY

Boost the happiness around you with these 101 feel-good sticky note surprises. You'll find unexpected compliments, thoughtful coupons, much-needed encouragement, lighthearted fun, and silly doodles to make anyone grin. Just tear them out and post wherever they'll be found by someone who needs a little lift. When you give a jolt of unexpected joy with these instant happy notes, get ready to feel happier yourself!

A
GOLD STAR
for you.

"Dwell in POSSIBILITY."

—Emily Dickinson

Congratulations!

YOU

deserve it!

You know what
you are? A

SUPERSTAR.

Happiness is...

1. _____

2. _____

3. _____

You made my

DAY.

"BE BOLD,
and mighty
forces will come
to your aid."
—*Goethe*

TGIF!

Flowers to
BRIGHTEN
your day.

"Even if **HAPPINESS** forgets you a little bit, never completely forget about it."

—*Jacques Prévert*

You've really

made a

DIFFERENCE!

THANKS

for all your help!

You
LOOK
GREAT
today!

There's nothing happier than a

HAPPY HOUR!

Wanna go?

Treat yourself to an **ICE CREAM** sundae. Something about sprinkles, hot fudge, and whipped cream can make anyone smile.

"The Constitution only guarantees the American people the right to pursue HAPPINESS. You have to catch it yourself."

—Benjamin Franklin

Where's your

HAPPY

PLACE?

THANKS
for everything.

You made me
SMILE
today.

Need an

EXCUSE

to smile? Try

dailypuppy.com

"The big secret in life is that there is no big SECRET. Whatever your goal, you can get there if you're willing to work."

—Oprah Winfrey

Have a

GREAT

day!

FIESTA
time!

A glass of
WINE can help
prevent heart
disease, cancer,
and more. Enjoy.

You didn't forget
CHOCOLATE
is good for you,
right? Enjoy!

Here's to
YOU!

You are one
of my
BLESSINGS.

Awesomeness
grade: A+

TO-DO LIST:

- ☐ Read
- ☐ Relax
- ☐ Bubble Bath
- ☐ Nap

Good for one
BIG HUG.
Anytime.

TGIF!

FRIENDS

make even
Mondays seem
happy.

Did you know that frowning uses more muscles than

SMILING?

Don't worry,
BE HAPPY.

Thanks for being
YOU!

If friends were
FLOWERS,
I'd pick you.

I think this
situation calls for
KARAOKE.

"Happiness
is not a
DESTINATION.
It is a method
of life."
—*Burton Hills*

Being with
you is having
the TIME
of my life.

Good morning,
SUNSHINE.

"Sanity and
HAPPINESS
are an impossible
combination."
—*Mark Twain*

You're

CUTE

as a button.

"I know GOD will not give me anything I can't handle. I just wish that He didn't trust me so much."

—*Mother Teresa*

Today is a
good day for a
PICNIC in the
park—let's not
waste it!

May all your
WISHES
come true.

Just for you, a
SUNNY DAY.

You make
everything
FUN!

You're pretty in
PINK!
And purple…and
green…and yellow…
and blue…and red…
and orange…

I love to
HEAR
your laugh.

Some things never get old. Permission to listen to your FAVORITE song on repeat!

TGIF!

CHOOSE
happy today.

Ten-second
vacation:
Think about
a trip to the
BEACH.

"Sometimes your joy is the source of **YOUR SMILE,** but sometimes your smile can be the source of your joy."

—*Thich Nhat Hanh*

Enjoy the

SIMPLE

things.

Kiss and hug;
forgive and
LOVE.

LAUGH OUT LOUD.

It increases your heart rate, can reduce stress, and fights infection.

COUNT
your blessings:

_____

_____

_____

_____

_____

Live.

Laugh.

Love.

REPEAT.

TGIF!

"HAPPINESS?
That's nothing
more than health
and a poor
memory."
—Albert Schweitzer

If you need
someone to
LISTEN,
I'm all ears.

Be **SILLY**
today.

Nothing turns
a bad mood
into a good
one faster than
CHOCOLATE.

"Don't frown, for you never know who is falling in LOVE with your smile."

—*Unknown*

NAPS
are highly
underrated.

Roses are red,
VIOLETS
ARE BLUE,
Today will get better;
This I promise you.

Let's get
some lunch.

MY TREAT.

If you're happy
and you know
it…SMILE!

"When it is dark enough, you can see the STARS."

—*Ralph Waldo Emerson*

You look like
you could use a
FRIEND.
I'm here.

Choose
JOY
today!

"Whoever is
HAPPY
will make others
happy too."
—*Mark Twain*

You're the
BEST.

"Most folks are about as happy as they make up their MINDS to be."

—*Abraham Lincoln*

Most problems don't look
so bad after a glass of
LEMONADE.

$e = mc^2$

REMINDER:
You are brilliant.

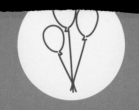

HANG
in there.

You
INSPIRE
me.

"It's not that I'm so
SMART,
it's just that I stay
with problems
longer."
—*Albert Einstein*

Can't wait to

SEE YOU

again.

"The purpose of LIFE is to be defeated by greater and greater things."
—Rainer Maria Rilke

Ten-second
VACATION:
Think about a
trip to the zoo.

BLUE

is very
calming. I wish
you an ocean of
chilling out.

CHERISH

the simple things.

This situation calls
for extra-large
COFFEES
with some sort of
bakery goodness.
Let's go.

You always
have such
BRIGHT
IDEAS.

I told you so:
You're
AMAZING.

Chocolate.
Graham Crackers.
MARSHMALLOWS.
Us. Now.

Why I'm
happy right now:
YOU.

Smile. Smile. Smile.

Smile. Smile. Smile.

Smile. Smile. Smile.

Smile. SMILE.

Smile. Smile. Smile.

Smile. Smile. Smile.

Play-Doh.
Sidewalk chalk.
FINGER PAINT.
Somehow they
make problems
seem less serious.

You:

~~Good~~

~~Better~~

BEST

You're a
GEM!

_____

_____

_____